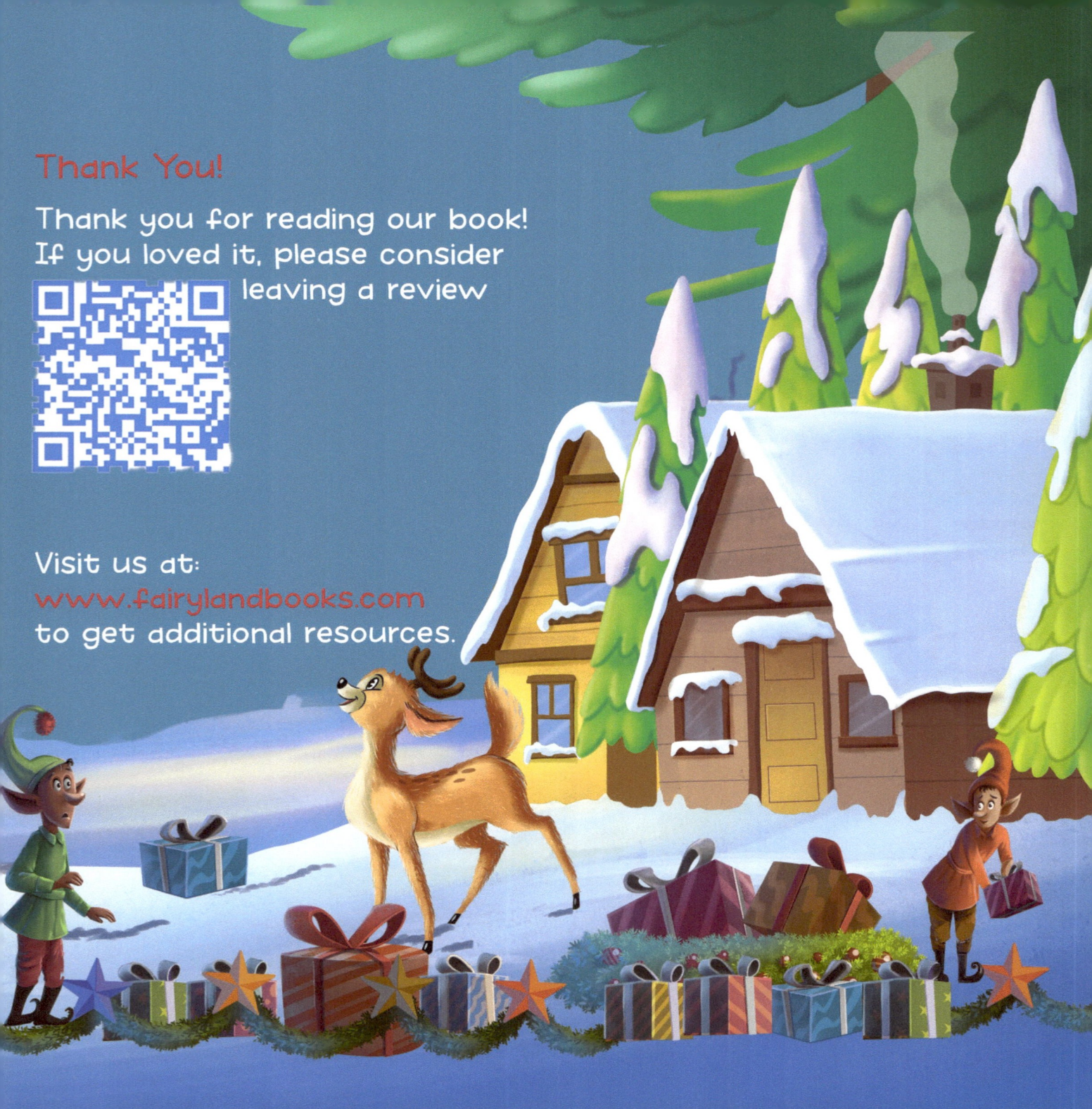

About the Author
Sue Elias

Sue Elias has always been fond of creating plays and stories and using her imagination to keep children engaged. As a teaching assistant for children with special needs, she understands the importance of reading fairytales, classics, and nicely illustrated children's books. Sue was born in Kuwait and now resides in Canada. Her first book, Sweet Dreams of Christmas, was released in 2022.

Illustrated by
Remesh Ram
Co Founder of Prayan Animation Studios

"I might be a little clumsy, but I'd love to help again next year," says Snowflake. "That's wonderful!" says Santa, patting Snowflake on this head.

Merry Christmas to all! See you next year!"

Snowflake helps the girl rebuild the snowman. The people of the town gather around. "Well done!" Santa says. "Your gift made the whole town happy."

IT'S EVEN BETTER!"
She hugs her new Dog-Elephant-Cat-Donkey tightly.

"Oh!" says the girl, opening her present. "It's not what I asked for...

"Ah! But... you already helped!" says Santa, jumping down from the sleigh.
He hands the girl her Christmas gift—the only one left.

"Oh. Jingle, jingle, jingle bells!" Snowflake mutters, hanging his head down. "I don't think I can help you."

"I knew you'd come!" A little girl rushes towards Snowflake.
I asked to bring me something special this year.
"She looks up and down and all around. "Where is Santa?"

He crashes...right into a big snowman!

Snowflake pulls hard, trying to turn the sleigh around.
His harness breaks and he tumbles towards the ground.

Snowflake hears someone crying.
He knows this must be the child who didn't get a present.
"I can help!" he says.

"We're finished!" Santa declares, as the sun rises in the sky.
"We need to go home.
Mrs. Claus is waiting with cookies and cocoa for everyone!"

"Oh! Jingle, jingle, jingle bells!" Snowflake mutters
They've been too busy for him to explain about the missing name,

They take off into the night sky.

Perfect! While they deliver gifts, he will tell Santa about the child's name that's smeared with cocoa.

But Snowflake is still trying to help Santa get through his tasks:

#4 Hitch the reindeer

"I know I can help!" Snowflake says.

"Snowflake, you will help pull the sleigh," Santa says.

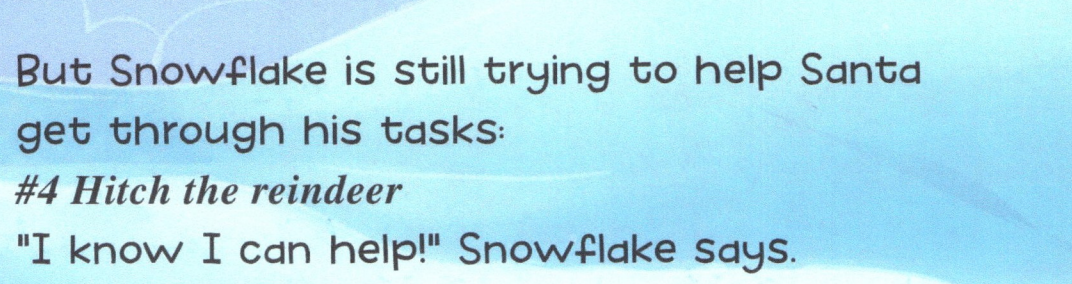

"Oh! Jingle, jingle, jingle bells," Snowflake mutters.
"My ankle is twisted," cries the older reindeer.
Santa runs in to see what's happening.
"Can you still fly?"
he asks the limping reindeer.
"No, I can't fly. I need to rest my leg,"
says the injured reindeer.
Santa looks worried.
What is he to do now?

Then Snowflake remembers Santa's tasks again:
#3 Load the Sleigh.
Snowflake rushes toward the barn, yelling, "I can help!"

He's rushing so fast
that he plows into another reindeer,
knocking him off his feet.

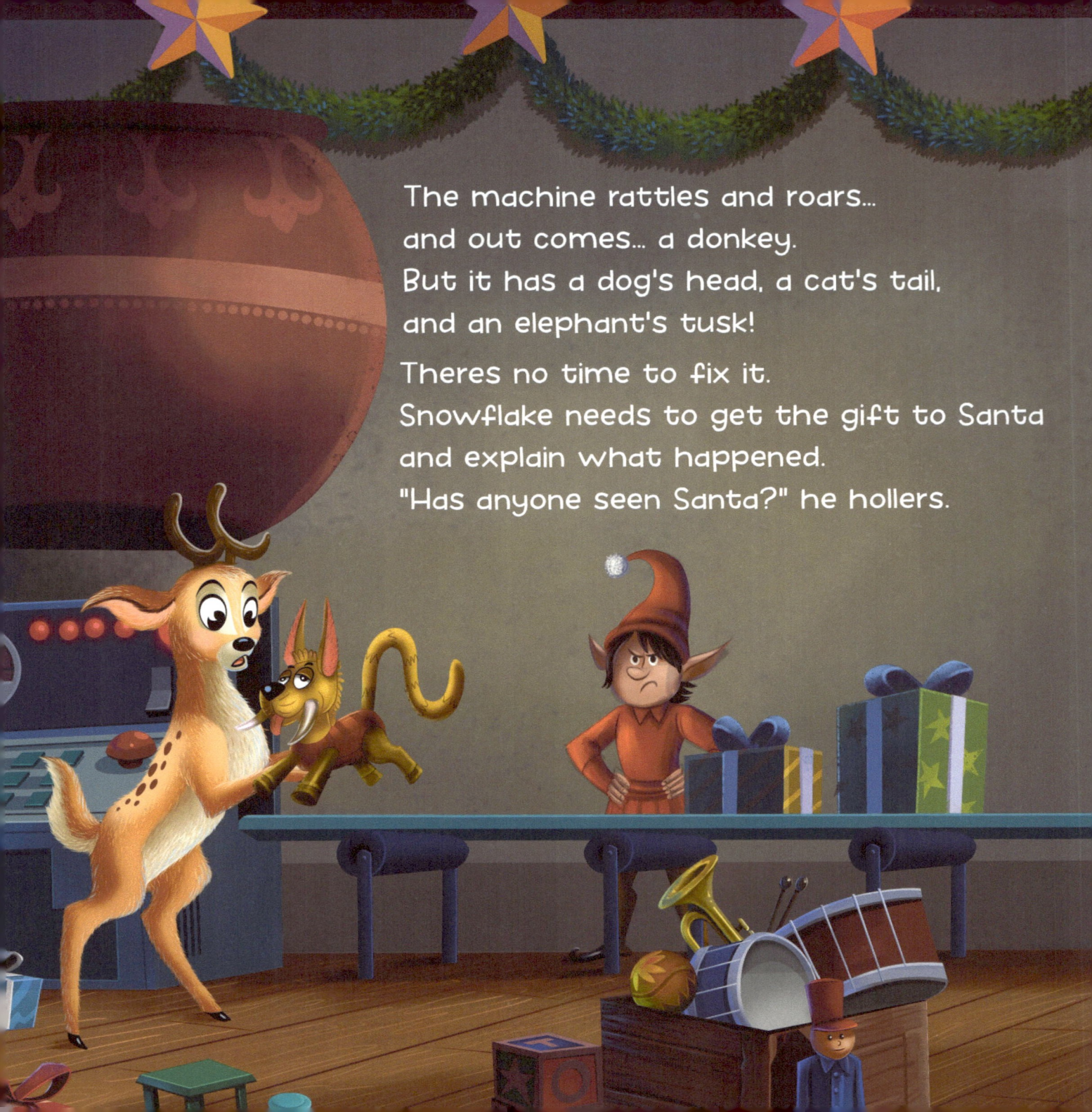

The machine rattles and roars...
and out comes... a donkey.
But it has a dog's head, a cat's tail,
and an elephant's tusk!

Theres no time to fix it.
Snowflake needs to get the gift to Santa
and explain what happened.
"Has anyone seen Santa?" he hollers.

The elves try to stop Snowflake.
They know he's not careful.

They are afraid he might break
the toy machine.
But Snowflake is determined.

When Snowflake arrives at the workshop,
the toy-making machine is turned off.
"Oh! Jingle, jingle, jingle bells," Snowflake mutters.
"I'm too late! There will be a child without a toy."
Snowflake looks at the machine and declares, "I can do this!"

"Oh! Jingle, jingle, jingle bells," Snowflake mutters. "Where did he go?"
Then Snowflake remembers Santa's tasks:

#2 Finish making the toys

"I can do that," Snowflake says, as he heads for Santa's workshop.
"But I still have to tell Santa about the list.
The child whose name is smeared won't get a toy."

"Snowflake!" says Santa, rushing in.
"You checked my list! Thank you so much."
"Santa! I--"Snowflake begins to explain.
But Santa gives him a loving pat on the head
and dashes a way.

Snowflake finds the list of names
of every child who will receive a gift.
He is so excited that he jumps up...
And spills a cup of cocoa that is sitting on Santa's desk.
"Oh! Jingle, jingle jingle bells." Snowflake mutters,
as warm cocoa drips all over Santa's desk.
"The last child's name is now smeared with cocoa.
Santa will never be able to read it."

"I can help" Snowflake says.
Snowflake is a helpful reindeer.
He tries hard, but he's not very careful.
He is always stumbling and dropping things.

The workshop is buzzing with excitement.
"I have so many things to do!"
says Santa. "I can't start the Christmas deliveries until everything is in order."
Santa makes a list of the important tasks that must be done.

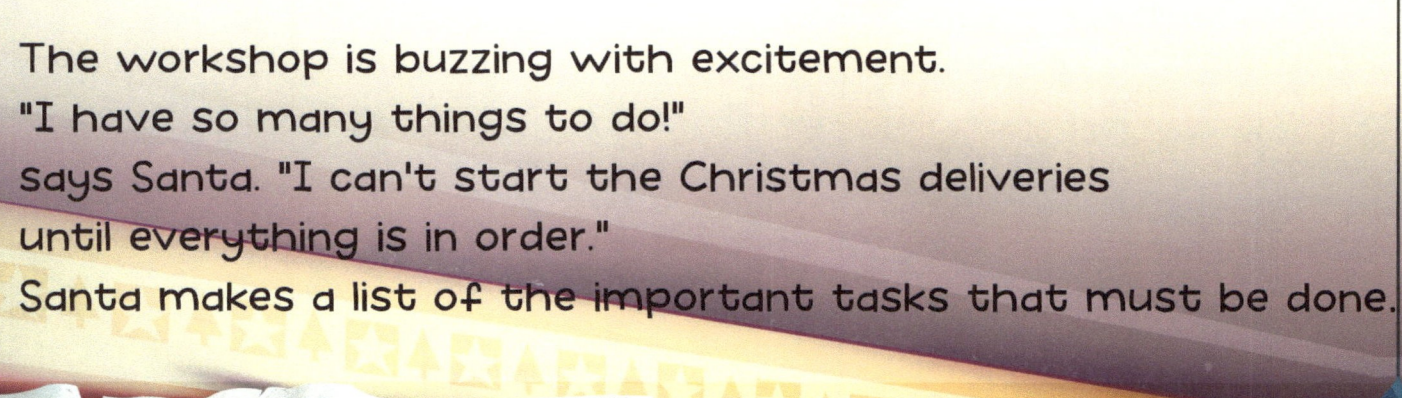

1. Check the list
2. Finish making the toys
3. Load the sleigh
4. Hitch the reindeer

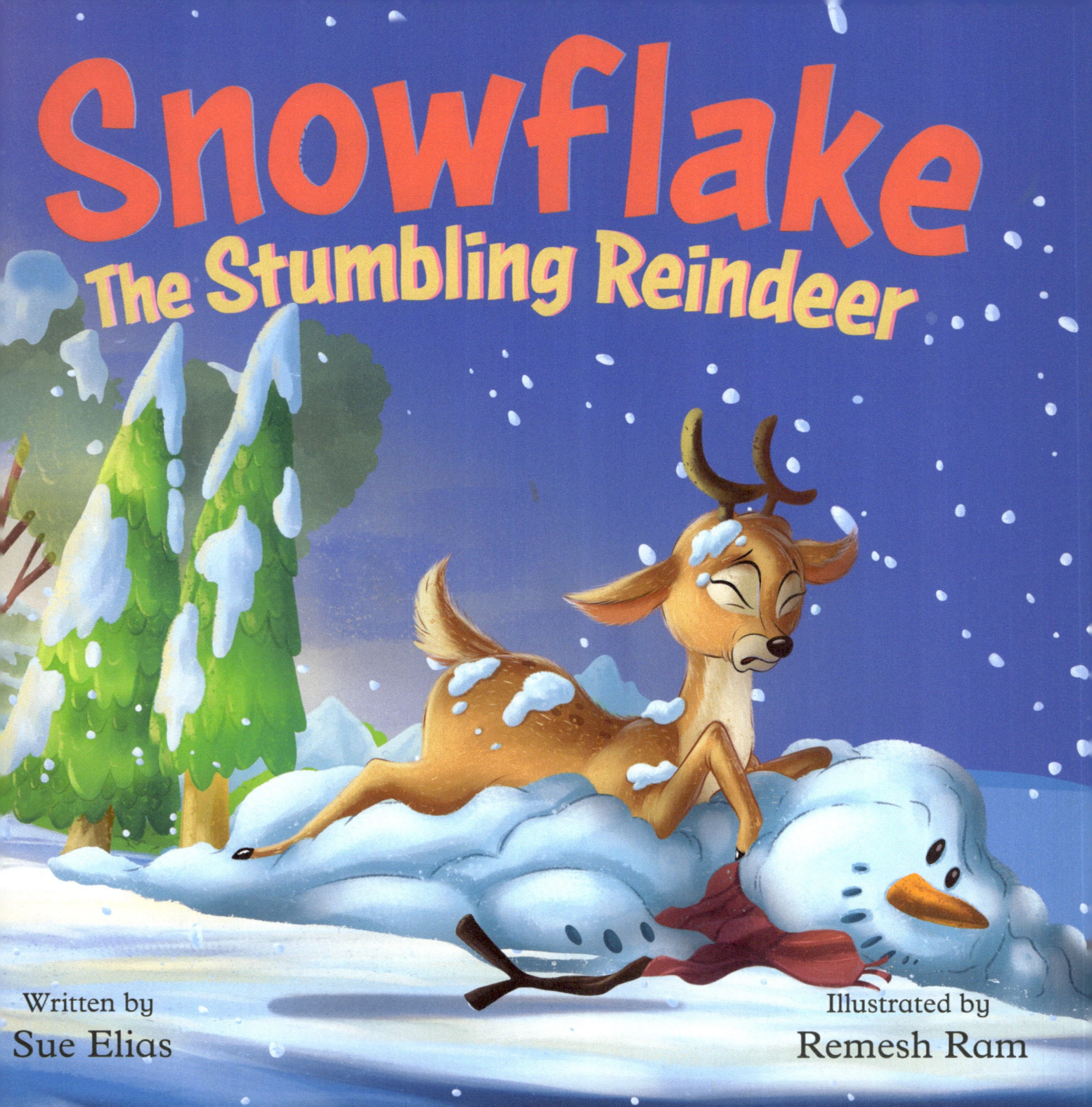

This book is dedicated with love to my husband, our wonderful kids and to Hanadi, Rania, and Jackie.

Special thanks to:
My editor, Bobbie Hinman: Bestfairybooks.com
and Tammy Lempert at The Complete Self-Publishing Services:
www.tammylempert.com

Copyright © 2023 Fairyland Books
All rights reserved.
No part of this publication may be used, reproduced, stored in a retrieval system or transmitted in any form or by any means, electronic, mechanical, photocopying, recording, scanning or otherwise, without the prior written permission from the publisher.
Illustrations by Prayan Animation Studio
Book Design by Tammy Lempert

Publisher's Cataloging-in-Publication data

Names: Elias, Sue, author. | Prayan Animation Studio, illustrator. | Remesh, Ram, illustrator.
Title: Snowflake the stumbling reindeer / written by Sue Elias; illustrations by Prayan Animation Studio; illustrated by Ram Remesh.
Description: Brampton, Ontario, Canada: Fairyland Books, 2023. |
Summary: A playful mishap with a mug of cocoa thrusts Snowflake the reindeer into an unexpected challenge that tests Snowflake's courage and uncovers his real potential to bring cheer in an unexpected way.
Identifiers: ISBN: 978-1-998058-01-3 (hardcover) | 978-1-998058-03-7 (paperback) | 978-1-998058-02-0 (ebook)

This book belongs to
_____

Printed in the USA
CPSIA information can be obtained
at www.ICGtesting.com
LVHW060555251123
764762LV00019B/631